TRANSFORM
YOUR LIFE

A YEAR OF AWARENESS PRACTICE

CHERI HUBER

AUTHOR OF THERE IS NOTHING WRONG WITH YOU

Also by Cheri Huber

From Keep It Simple Books
Transform Your Life: A Year of Awareness Practice
There Is Nothing Wrong With You: Going Beyond Self-Hate, Rev. Ed.
The Key and the Name of the Key Is Willingness
That Which You Are Seeking Is Causing You to Seek
How You Do Anything Is How You Do Everything: A Workbook
There Is Nothing Wrong With You for Teens
The Depression Book: Depression/Opportunity for Spiritual Growth
The Fear Book: Facing Fear Once and for All
Nothing Happens Next: Responses to Questions about Meditation
Be the Person You Want to Find: Relationship and Self-Discovery
Suffering Is Optional: Three Keys to Freedom and Joy
When You're Falling, Dive: Acceptance, Possibility and Freedom
Time-Out for Parents: A Guide to Compassionate Parenting, Rev. Ed.
Trying to Be Human: Zen Talks (Sara Jenkins, editor)
Good Life: Zen Precepts Retreat with Cheri Huber (Sara Jenkins, editor)
Buddha Facing the Wall (Sara Jenkins, editor)
Sweet Zen: Dharma Talks with Cheri Huber (Sara Jenkins, editor)
This Side of Nirvana (Sara Jenkins, editor)
The Zen Monastery Cookbook: Stories and Recipes from a Zen Kitchen

From Shambhala Publications
Making a Change for Good: A Guide to Compassionate Self-Discipline

From Hay House
How to Get from Where You Are to Where You Want to Be

From Sounds True
Unconditional Self-Acceptance: A Do-It-Yourself Course (6 CD set)

— — —

DVDs from Openings (www.yogaopenings.com)
There Are No Secrets: Zen Meditation with Cheri Huber
Yoga for Meditators - *Christa Rypins*
Yoga for a Better Back - *Christa Rypins and Dr. John Sousa*
Yummy Yoga: Stress Relief for Hips, Back, and Neck - *Christa Rypins*

ISBN: 0-9710309-5-2
ISBN13: 9780971030954

Published by Keep It Simple Books

Printed in the United States of America

Illustrations by Alex Mill
Cover design by Mary Denkinger
sunwheelart@earthlink.net

First printing: October 2007

Introduction

"Awareness practice" is *practicing* living in conscious compassionate *awareness* rather than identifying the antics of conditioned mind as yourself. As a child, when you were being socialized, you learned to think, feel, say and do specific things relative to circumstances. "Conditioned mind" is the endless stream of habitual thoughts that go through your head as a result of being socialized. We weren't all socialized the same, obviously, but we did all learn to react to life in ways that, we believed, would ensure survival. Now, as adults, we are still reacting to life from a child's survival system - we are still surviving childhood!

Believing that "who you are" is your conditioned mind (your thoughts and reactions

to life learned in childhood) is an enormous
hindrance to living authentically in the
moment. Awareness practice is the process
of discovering those
no-longer-helpful
reactions, dropping
them, and living free
and joyously.

In lovingkindness,
Cheri

HOW TO USE THIS BOOK

Read day by day; don't read ahead.

Do each assignment in turn.

Write down the day's assignment and take it with you.

ENCOURAGEMENTS

Use reminders - screensavers, a vibrating watch, a special bracelet or ring, etc.

Enroll your friends and follow this book as a group.

Keep a journal of awareness.

If you quit, start again.

Repeat each year.

The blessings of love and respect we offer to all, in times past and present, who have opened the doors of wisdom, reuniting all beings with their intrinsic purity.
--second bead, The Daily Recollection

January 1

What you are looking for is who is looking.
--St. Francis of Assisi

Our way of saying that is "that which you are seeking is causing you to seek," which is the title of one of our books. Our deepest

heart's desire, our authentic nature, is drawing us home. What you are looking for is doing the looking. The guidance you seek is guiding you.

ASSIGNMENT: Today, allow yourself to sense that which has been guiding you back to your heart.

January 2

You can search throughout the entire universe for someone who is more deserving of your love and affection than you are yourself, and that person is not to be found anywhere. You yourself, as much as anybody in the entire universe, deserve your love and affection.
--The Buddha

ASSIGNMENT: Today, allow yourself to consider that you, just as you are, are as deserving as any other person of your love and affection. (Extra credit: Notice if you hear any opinions to the contrary.)

January 3

Wherever you are is the entry point.
--Kabir

Many of us have been taught to believe that we must first complete rigorous efforts at self-improvement before we will be worthy to attempt something as lofty as awareness practice or spiritual practice. Not so. Wherever you are is the perfect place to begin--anything!

ASSIGNMENT: Today, notice that you have already begun to practice awareness at a deeper lever than before.

January 4

To live is so startling it leaves little time
for anything else.
--Emily Dickinson

Control, which is only an illusion, is over
rated. Life has much better ideas for us
than we could ever imagine for ourselves.

ASSIGNMENT: Today, allow yourself to be
startled by life.

January 5

The first problem for all of us is not to learn, but to unlearn.
--Gloria Steinem

Unexamined beliefs, assumptions, false notions, superstitions, magical thinking, erroneous opinions--these are just a few of the things that keep us from being present to what is.

ASSIGNMENT: Today, stop three times and notice which of the above your mind was engaged in while left on its own.

January 6

Normal is not something to aspire to; it's something to get away from.
--Jodie Foster

ASSIGNMENT: Today, try not to be normal. Hint: Normal for you is something you have defined.

January 7

There is only one great adventure and that is inwards towards the self.
--Henry Miller

ASSIGNMENT: Today, sit for a few moments with your favorite beverage and consider your embarkation on this current phase of your great adventure inwards toward the self.

January 8

Condition: in psychology, to cause to respond
in a certain way to a certain stimulus; to
develop a reflex or behavior pattern.
Conditioned: in philosophy or metaphysics,
that which depends upon or is determined by
something else; opposed to the absolute.
--Webster's New Universal Unabridged
Dictionary

Children are taught everything - what to
think and feel, what everything means, how
to behave, how to react to life - everything!

ASSIGNMENT: Today, notice some of the
ways you have been conditioned to react to
life.

January 9

Egocentric:

1) dwelling upon one's self or upon one's own personal interests almost to the exclusion of everything else; viewing everything in relation to oneself; self-centered.

2) in philosophy, existing only as conceived in the individual mind.

--Webster's New Universal Unabridged Dictionary

ASSIGNMENT: Today, be aware of some of the ways conditioning results in egocentricity. Example: I'm in a hurry; I shouldn't have to wait for slow people. (Extra credit: Remember that conditioning and egocentricity is universal and not to be taken personally.)

January 10

The words "I am..." are potent words; be careful what you hitch them to. The thing you're claiming has a way of reaching back and claiming you.
--A. K. Kitselman

A simple example of this is the difference between "I am ____(your name)," and "My name is ____."

ASSIGNMENT: Today, notice what you have unconsciously claimed and the hold that claim has on you.

January 11

A happy life must be to a great extent a quiet life, for it is only in an atmosphere of quiet that true joy can live.
--Bertrand Russell

ASSIGNMENT: Today, find some quiet moments for yourself.

January 12

Nothing great was ever achieved without enthusiasm.
--Ralph Waldo Emerson

The Random House College Dictionary defines enthusiasm as "lively, absorbing interest; excited involvement."

ASSIGNMENT: Today, develop an absorbing interest in whether or not you have a tendency to curb your enthusiasm. If you do have that tendency, enthusiastically drop it, thereby achieving something great.

January 13

Who looks outside, dreams; who looks inside, awakes.
--Carl Gustav Jung

ASSIGNMENT: Today, notice how your awareness increases when you observe yourself.

January 14

Freedom is like taking a bath -- you have to keep doing it every day!
--Florynce Kennedy

A big part of awareness practice is becoming aware of, and getting free of, what we were taught as children to believe that is not true, and perhaps never was.

ASSIGNMENT: Today, notice when an unexamined belief robs you of freedom.

January 15

The other side of every fear is a freedom.
--Marilyn Ferguson

The quickest way to find the freedom on the other side of fear is to stop running from the fear, turn around, open your arms, and invite it in.

ASSIGNMENT: Today, notice "who" you have to be to have the courage to embrace that which you fear. Choose something you've been running from - start small - and embrace it.

January 16

What one takes in by contemplation, one pours out in love.
--Meister Eckhart

ASSIGNMENT: Today, look to see if finding some moments of quiet (find a beautiful, quiet place to have them if you can) helps you be more patient.

January 17

Meditation is not a difficult task. It is a way to lead you to your long-lost home.
--Soen Shaku

ASSIGNMENT: Today, consider that meditation is nothing more complex than sitting still with your own heart.

January 18

A meditation hall is not a place for bliss and relaxation, but a furnace room for the combustion of our egoistic delusions. What tools do we need to use? Only one. We've all heard of it, yet we use it very seldom. It's called attention.
--Charlotte Joko Beck

Attention moves in the field of awareness much like a spotlight in a lighted room. Awareness illuminates the world (inside and out), attention spotlights the various content.

ASSIGNMENT: Today, consciously move your attention from thing to thing while remaining aware that you're doing so.

January 19

Silence is the essential condition of
happiness.
--Heinrich Heine

ASSIGNMENT: Today, explore your
relationship with silence.

January 20

The truth dazzles gradually, or else the
world would be blind.
--Emily Dickinson

ASSIGNMENT: Today, notice those little
moments of insight that "dazzle."

January 21

Expect nothing, live frugally on surprise.
--Alice Walker

I suspect Ms. Walker's use of "frugally" in this sentence is meant to suggest the opposite.

ASSIGNMENT: Today, be open to surprise, even if it feels uncomfortable.

January 22

Do not think you will necessarily be aware of
your own enlightenment.
--Dogen

From what we hear or read about
enlightenment, it can seem very different
from our own lives. Enlightenment is a
description of our authentic nature. The
fact that we are not attending to it does
not mean it is not there.

ASSIGNMENT: Today, remind yourself that
you cannot know where you are along the
path to awakening--comparisons and
judgments only hinder us.

January 23

The curious paradox is that when I accept
myself just as I am, then I can change.
--Carl Rogers

ASSIGNMENT: Today, recall examples of this
fact from your own life. Make a list.

January 24

Do not be afraid.

--Jesus

The truth is there is nothing to fear.

ASSIGNMENT: Today, consider the role fear plays in your life. (Remember judgments only slow us down - internal judgment even more than external judgment.)

January 25

How we spend our days is, of course, how
we spend our lives.
--Annie Dillard

This refers to *process*, not *content*. It's not
a matter of *what* you do, it's *how* you are
as you do it.

ASSIGNMENT: Today, spend a little time
being how you want your life to be.

January 26

Whether you think that you can, or that you can't, you are usually right.
--Henry Ford

ASSIGNMENT: Today, let yourself become aware of one thing your conditioning says you can't do that you are now open to doing.

January 27

This is your time, your world, your pleasure.
--William Stafford

ASSIGNMENT: Today, realize that now is the
time, here is the place. Take a breath and
feel the pleasure.

January 28

It is only possible to live happily ever after on a day-to-day basis.
--Margaret Bonnano

ASSIGNMENT: Today, consider what "happily ever after" means to you. Can you have a little of that today?

January 29

We turn to God for help when our foundations are shaking, only to learn that it is God who is shaking them.
--Charles C. West

ASSIGNMENT: What has been "shaking" you that you might be ready to see as a spiritual opportunity?

January 30

In Oriental cultures, they don't think of God as an autocrat. God is the fundamental energy of the world, which performs all this world without having to think about it.
--Alan Watts

ASSIGNMENT: Today, whenever you think of it, turn your attention to the little gaps between the thoughts.

January 31

Faith is like electricity. You can't see it, but you can see the light.
--Author Unknown

ASSIGNMENT: Today, acknowledge that you are seeing the light.

February 1

If the only prayer you said in your whole life
was, "thank you," that would suffice.
--Meister Eckhart

ASSIGNMENT: Today, say "thank you" every
chance you get. Notice how that feels.

February 2

Saying thank you is more than good
manners. It is good spirituality.
--Alfred Painter

ASSIGNMENT: Today, continue saying "thank
you" as often as you can and add a smile.

February 3

A diamond is just a lump of coal that stuck to its job.
--Leonardo da Vinci

ASSIGNMENT: Today, recognize that "lump of coal" in your life that you suspect is a diamond in the making if only you will stick with it.

February 4

You've got to jump off cliffs all the time
and build your wings on the way down.
--Annie Dillard

ASSIGNMENT: Today, unpack that "wing
building" kit.

February 5

You are fooled by your mind into believing
there is tomorrow, so you may waste today.
--Ishin Yoshimoto

ASSIGNMENT: Today, consider what you
would do, how you would be, if this were
your last day.

February 6

There came a time when the risk to remain tight in the bud was more painful than the risk it took to blossom.
--Anais Nin

ASSIGNMENT: Today, consider one place in your life where you remain tight but would like to blossom.

February 7

If you have always done it that way, it is
probably wrong.
--Charles Kettering

So much of what we do is an unconscious,
unexamined reaction to everything that has
happened to us, especially in childhood. As we
begin to wake up to the pain and suffering
of rejections, disappointments, and hurts, it
is tempting to find fault and assign blame. It
is important to acknowledge what happened,
but to stay stuck in the past simply destroys
our present.

ASSIGNMENT: Today, recognize your
conditioned reactions for what they are and
remind yourself you can let them go.

February 8

It is not the strongest of the species that survives, nor the most intelligent, but the one most responsive to change.
--Charles Darwin

ASSIGNMENT: Today, change one small habit and watch what happens.

February 9

Three things in human life are important.
The first is to be kind. The second is to be
kind. The third is to be kind.
--Henry James

ASSIGNMENT: Today, notice kindness
wherever you encounter it.

February 10

You gain strength, courage, and confidence by every experience in which you really stop to look fear in the face. You must do the thing which you think you cannot do.
--Eleanor Roosevelt

ASSIGNMENT: Today, make a list of the things you fear. Which one would you choose to engage in order to begin facing fear?

February 11

I'm not afraid of storms, for I'm learning
how to sail my ship.
--Louisa May Alcott

So much of our conditioning convinces us
that only "knowing" and "being right" matter.
If we must learn something, that's proof we
don't know and are therefore wrong. But
learning, making peace with not knowing, is
not being wrong, it is the path to freedom.
Excitement is another word for the
sensations we think of as fear.

ASSIGNMENT: Today, feel the excitement of
considering doing something "dangerous" that
you have always wanted to do.

February 12

Worry gives a small thing a big shadow.
--Swedish proverb

We have a t-shirt that reads, "Worry is not preparation." Conditioned mind keeps our lives small by making us afraid. "What if ____ happened? That would be awful." The vast majority of what conditioning wants us to be afraid of and worry about never happens.

ASSIGNMENT: Today, observe the voices of worry talking to you.

February 13

Freedom is what you do with what's been done to you.
--Jean-Paul Sartre

In the present we can undo the past and release the future. Horrible things may have happened in the past, but we don't owe those horrible things our present or our future. If the voices re-telling the story could change it, that might be worthwhile. But they can't. Only we can reclaim our precious now by letting go the old stories. You can use your past as strength for your present.

ASSIGNMENT: Today, look to see which old story you are ready to bless and release.

February 14

The best way out is always through.
--Robert Frost

We can waste a life trying to avoid. If we
shrink enough, we won't be a big target. If
we ignore something, maybe it will go away.
It doesn't work. How do we know that? It
hasn't.

ASSIGNMENT: Today, remind yourself that
you are on a hero's journey and that you're
a hero for having started and for continuing.

February 15

If we did the things we are capable of, we would astound ourselves.
--Thomas Alva Edison

If we simply acknowledged all that we are currently doing, we would astound ourselves!

ASSIGNMENT: Today, bring some conscious awareness to all you are currently doing.

February 16

Never give up and never face the facts.
--Ruth Gordon

ASSIGNMENT: Today, notice what lies you've been taught to believe are facts. Ask yourself regularly throughout the day, "Is that true?" "How do I know that's true?"

February 17

The next message you need is always right
where you are.
--Ram Dass

ASSIGNMENT: Today, look around. What's
the message?

February 18

When they tell you to grow up, they mean
stop growing.
--Tom Robbins

ASSIGNMENT: Today, recall something you
used to love to do but gave up to be a
grown up. Make a date to do it.

February 19

There is no coming to consciousness without pain.
--C. G. Jung

ASSIGNMENT: Today, smile each time you see the color red. (Take a long, deep breath and feel the pain melt away.)

February 20

Argue for your limitations, and sure enough, they're yours.
--Richard Bach

ASSIGNMENT: Today, smile each time you see the color orange. (Can you feel the limitations falling away?)

February 21

Your pain is the breaking of the shell that encloses your understanding.
--Kahlil Gibran

ASSIGNMENT: Today, smile each time you see the color yellow. (Can you feel that shell breaking?)

February 22

Everybody is all right really.
--Winnie the Pooh

ASSIGNMENT: Today, smile each time you
see the color green. (Remind yourself that
everybody is all right really.)

February 23

Joy is not in things; it is in us.
--Richard Wagner

ASSIGNMENT: Today, smile each time you
see the color blue. (Can you feel the joy?)

February 24

Millions of people long for immortality who
do not know what to do with themselves on
a rainy afternoon.
--Susan Ertz

ASSIGNMENT: Today, smile each time you
see the color purple. (Take a deep breath,
and feel the tension release.)

February 25

Rest does not come from sleeping but from waking.
--A Course In Miracles

ASSIGNMENT: Today, smile each time you see white. Very restful!

February 26

The problem is not that there are problems. The problem is expecting otherwise and thinking that having problems is a problem.
--Theodore Isaac Rubin

ASSIGNMENT: Today, notice the solutions rather than the problems.

February 27

Always be a little kinder than necessary.
--James Barrie

ASSIGNMENT: Today, be a whole lot kinder
to yourself than you had imagined possible.

February 28

Life is uncertain. Eat dessert first.
--Ernestine Ulmer

Why do we want dessert? We want dessert because dessert is pleasurable, sweet, and enjoyable. It is possible always to have pleasurable, sweet, and enjoyable first in life, if we do not confuse that pleasure, sweetness, or enjoyment with content or food. Every moment to which we are present is pleasurable, sweet, and enjoyable.

ASSIGNMENT: Today, have dessert first.

(This exercise is so pleasurable, sweet and enjoyable, for leap year do it again!)

March 1

As you look at many people's lives, you see that their suffering is in a way gratifying, for they are comfortable in it. They make their lives a living hell, but a familiar one.
--Ram Dass

ASSIGNMENT: Today, take a look at some of the familiar, comfortable hells that plague you.

March 2

If you stop to be kind you must swerve
often from your path.
--Mary Webb

ASSIGNMENT: Today, swerve a little for
kindness's sake.

March 3

We must be holy without holiness. We must be whole, complete. That's being holy. Any other kind of holiness is false, a snare, and a delusion.
--Henry Miller

ASSIGNMENT: Today, without judgment or conclusions, consider ways in which you could be more whole.

Love until it hurts.
--Mother Teresa

ASSIGNMENT: Today, practice allowing your love to grow and expand. Love anyone or anything. Find the willingness to risk the growing pains.

March 5

Love is a condition in which the happiness of another person is essential to your own.
--Robert Heinlein

ASSIGNMENT: Today, find a way to bring happiness to another - for the love of it!

March 6

Be kind. Everyone you meet is fighting a
hard battle.
--John Watson

ASSIGNMENT: Today, see if you can
recognize the "hard battle" being fought by
everyone you meet. Hint: Notice eyes and
body language and the set of the mouth.

March 7

If you want others to be happy, practice
compassion. If you want to be happy,
practice compassion.
--The Dalai Lama

ASSIGNMENT: Today, look for compassion;
explore what compassion feels like to you.

March 8

My life is my message.
--Mahatma Gandhi

ASSIGNMENT: Today, consider if that is
true for you, and, if so, what is the
message of your life? (No hateful messages
from the voices of conditioning, please.)

March 9

Eternity is not the hereafter. Eternity has nothing to do with time. This is it. If you don't get it here, you won't get it anywhere. The experience of eternity right here and now is the function of life. Heaven is not the place to have the experience; here's the place to have the experience.
--Joseph Campbell

ASSIGNMENT: Today, let yourself have some experiences of heaven here and now.

March 10

The epitome of the human realm is to be stuck in a huge traffic jam of discursive thought.
--Chogyam Trungpa

ASSIGNMENT: Today, focus on the breaks in the traffic.

March 11

Zen does not confuse spirituality with
thinking about God while one is peeling
potatoes. Zen spirituality is just to peel the
potatoes.
--Alan Watts

ASSIGNMENT: Today, practice "just peeling
the potatoes" in whatever you're doing.

March 12

Everyone is in the best seat.
--John Cage

ASSIGNMENT: Today, remember that now is
the best time and here is the best place
for you to wake up and end suffering.

March 13

You yourselves must make the exertion. The Buddhas are only teachers.
--The Buddha

ASSIGNMENT: Today, remind yourself that no matter how many maps you read, you must make the journey. Remind yourself often that you are equal to the task.

March 14

Let us go singing as far as we go: the road
will be less tedious.
--Virgil

ASSIGNMENT: Today, sing with every step.

March 15

Kind words can be short and easy to speak
but their echoes are truly endless.
--Mother Teresa

ASSIGNMENT: Today, offer some of those
short, easy-to-speak kind words and enjoy
the echo.

March 16

One can pay back the loan of gold, but one lives forever in debt to those who are kind.
--Malayan proverb

Kindness is a debt that can be repaid only with the same coin.

ASSIGNMENT: Today, pay back as much kindness as possible.

March 17

I always prefer to believe the best of everybody; it saves so much trouble.
--Rudyard Kipling

ASSIGNMENT: Today, enjoy some of the time and energy saved by eschewing judgment and criticism.

March 18

Problems cannot be solved at the same level of awareness that created them.
--Albert Einstein

The voices of conditioning mind would have you hear the same stories and rehash the same problems endlessly, not because this leads to a solution but because it produces suffering.

ASSIGNMENT: Today, let yourself have some time-out from habitual conversations about problems and be open to the new level of awareness that can solve the problems.

March 19

There is nothing you need to do first in order to be enlightened.
--Thaddeus Golas

ASSIGNMENT: Today, each time you remember the quote, take a long, full breath and enjoy your inherent enlightenment.

March 20

What we see depends mainly on what we look for.
--John Lubbock

That explains a lot about how life works, doesn't it? I get what I get in life because that's what I'm open to getting, not because what I get is the only thing there is to get.

ASSIGNMENT: Today, look for joy.

March 21

Many of life's failures are people who did not realize how close they were to success when they gave up.
--Thomas Edison

ASSIGNMENT: Today, decide what in life you will not give up on. (No need to limit your list.)

March 22

The person who makes no mistakes does not usually make anything.
--Edward John Phelps

ASSIGNMENT: Today, make at least one colossal mistake and enjoy it thoroughly.

March 23

At 20 we worry about what others think of
us; at 40, we don't care what they think of
us; at 60, we discover they haven't been
thinking of us at all.
--Bob Hope

ASSIGNMENT: Today, be you as if no is
watching.

March 24

It is not healthy to be thinking all the time.
Thinking is intended for acquiring knowledge
or applying it. It is not essential living.
--Ernest Wood

ASSIGNMENT: Today, practice not thinking.
Hint: Attend to the spaces between the
thoughts rather than the thoughts.

March 25

What would people think about if people
weren't taught what to think about?
--Arthur Morgan

ASSIGNMENT: Today, don't think about that.
Today, think about not thinking. Then think
not-thinking.

March 26

Having precise ideas often leads to a person doing nothing.
--Paul Valery

ASSIGNMENT: Today, notice an area of your life in which your ideas are so "precise" that they have become limits to action.

.

March 27

Words, like eyeglasses, blur everything they
do not make clear.
--Joseph Joubert

ASSIGNMENT: Today, practice saying only
what is necessary - and kind!

March 28

Live the questions now. Perhaps then,
someday, far in the future, you will
gradually, without even noticing it, live your
way into the answer.
--Rainer Maria Rilke

ASSIGNMENT: Today, make a list of the
questions you have already lived into the
answers for. Notice if the answers have
created more questions.

March 29

The snowflakes fall, each in their proper
place.
--Zen saying

ASSIGNMENT: Today, be open to the
possibility that you, like the snowflakes, are
in the perfect place always.

March 30

Nothing can bring you peace but yourself.
--Ralph Waldo Emerson

ASSIGNMENT: Today, take a break from all concern, worry, striving, and effort. Ahhhh. Peace.

March 31

I do not want the peace that passeth understanding. I want the understanding which bringeth peace.
--Helen Keller

ASSIGNMENT: Today, consider what you would need to understand to find peace. For a few moments, drop that need and feel the peace.

April 1

Wherever there is a human being, there is a chance for a kindness.
--Seneca

ASSIGNMENT: Today, don't limit your kindness to human beings.

April 2

A kind word is like a spring day.
--Russian proverb

ASSIGNMENT: Today, bring someone a
spring day with your kind words.

April 3

Deeds of kindness are equal in weight to all the commandments.
--Talmud

ASSIGNMENT: Today, see how all the commandments point to kindness.

April 4

O snail,
Climb Mt. Fuji,
But slowly, slowly!
--Issa

ASSIGNMENT: Today, go at your own pace,
the pace that brings you peace.

April 5

When we are unable to find tranquility within ourselves, it is useless to seek it elsewhere.
--Francois de la Rochefoucauld

ASSIGNMENT: Today, decide how many tranquil moments you will give yourself and then have them.

April 6

Each moment is a place you've never been.
--Mark Strand

ASSIGNMENT: Today, spend as many moments as possible in awareness that this moment is a place you've never been.

April 7

I want to sing like birds sing
Not worrying about who hears or what they
think.
--Jelaluddin Rumi

ASSIGNMENT: Today put your whole heart
into what you would do if no one were
watching.

April 8

Many eyes go through the meadow, but few
see the flowers in it.
--Ralph Waldo Emerson

ASSIGNMENT: Today, see the flowers.

April 9

See into life. Don't just look at it.
--Anne Baxter

ASSIGNMENT: Today, look deeply into an ordinary part of your life you usually fail to see.

April 10

Words are the fog one has to see through.
--Zen saying

ASSIGNMENT: Today, find the words that come from the heart and follow them home.

The way to make your dreams come true is
to wake up.
--Paul Jackson

ASSIGNMENT: Today, every time you see
the color green, remind yourself to wake up.

April 12

You become what you think about all day long.
--Ralph Waldo Emerson

ASSIGNMENT: Today, without allowing voices of self-hate to give an opinion, consider what your daily thoughts are turning you into.

April 13

Kindness can become its own motive. We are made kind by being kind.
--Eric Hoffer

ASSIGNMENT: Today, practice deepening your kindness habit.

April 14

All truths are easy to understand once they are discovered; the point is to discover them.
--Galileo

Truth is an interesting notion, isn't it? We seem to lack evidence that there is any such thing as a truth that is true everywhere all the time. And yet, in any given moment, we might have an insight that shows us what is true for us now.

ASSIGNMENT: Today, consider what "truths" you have discovered for yourself.

April 15

Today I bent the truth to be kind, and I have no regret, for I am far surer of what is kind than I am of what is true.
--Robert Brault.

ASSIGNMENT: Today, let yourself choose kindness over "truth."

April 16

To dare is to lose one's footing momentarily. To not dare is to lose oneself.
--Soren Kierkegaard

ASSIGNMENT: Today, what will you dare in order not to lose yourself?

April 17

The best portion of a good person's life,
Those little, nameless, unremembered acts
Of kindness and love.
--William Wordsworth

The voices of conditioning would have us remember only that which is difficult, painful, and disappointing. Are there actually more of these than "little, nameless, unremembered acts of kindness and love"? Probably not, though the voices would wish us to believe that is so.

ASSIGNMENT: Today, let yourself have two of those little acts, one for you and one for someone else.

April 18

A thankful person is thankful under all circumstances. A complaining soul complains even while living in paradise.
--Bahu'u'llah

We're taught to feel bad about ourselves when we become aware of something about us that is less than ideal. But awareness is wisdom and clarity; it does not matter *what* one is aware of.

ASSIGNMENT: Today, see how you have been able to complain even in paradise. Let yourself be thankful for the awareness.

April 19

There are never enough "I love yous."
--Lenny Bruce

ASSIGNMENT: Today, say "I love you" at least ten times.

April 20

Besides the noble art of getting things done, there is the noble art of leaving things undone. The wisdom of life consists in the elimination of non-essentials.
--Lin Yutang

Much of our lives are spent doing things we don't want to do that don't need to be done.

ASSIGNMENT: Today, look for non-essentials you can eliminate. Hint: Look for the non-essentials in habits.

April 21

You make a living by what you get. You make a life by what you give.
--Winston Churchill

ASSIGNMENT: Today, give something "for your life." Let yourself receive that giving.

April 22

Money is like manure, it's not worth a thing unless it's spread around encouraging young things to grow.
--Thornton Wilder

ASSIGNMENT: Today, look to see what young things you want to grow with your money.

April 23

The habit of giving only enhances the desire to give.
--Walt Whitman

ASSIGNMENT: Today, look to see if you would like to enhance the desire to give and what you would like to give to accomplish that.

April 24

Perhaps everything terrible is in its deepest
being something helpless that wants help
from us.
--Rainer Maria Rilke

ASSIGNMENT: Today, consider what
"terrible thing" you would like to help.

April 25

It is better to give and receive.
--Bernard Gunther

ASSIGNMENT: Today, allow yourself to
receive your giving.

April 26

Kindness is more important than wisdom, and the recognition of this is the beginning of wisdom.
--Theodore Isaac Rubin

ASSIGNMENT: Today, look for evidence of this fact.

April 27

You will never be happy if you continue to search for what happiness consists of. You will never live if you are looking for the meaning of life.
--Albert Camus

It would seem that once again we are encouraged to prove to ourselves that everything we seek is available to us *here, now.*

ASSIGNMENT: Today, stop several times, turn your attention to the breath, relax as much as possible and *receive.*

April 28

We who lived in concentration camps can remember those who walked through the huts comforting others, giving away their last piece of bread. They may have been few in number, but they offer sufficient proof that everything can be taken away from a person but one thing: the last of the human freedoms - to choose one's attitude in any given set of circumstances, to choose one's own way.
--Viktor Frankl

ASSIGNMENT: Today, give yourself some quiet and solitude to consider the magnitude of that statement.

April 29

We cannot choose WHETHER to engage with the world, only HOW to.
--Stephen Batchelor

ASSIGNMENT: Today, look at HOW you engage with the world. Encouragement: Do not look to the voices of conditioning to answer this question.

April 30

Don't change the world, change worlds.
--Francis of Assisi

ASSIGNMENT: Today, consider what worlds
you would like to change.

May 1

The truest greatness lies in being kind, the truest wisdom in a happy mind.
--Ella Wheeler Wilcox

That sounds so simple, doesn't it?

ASSIGNMENT: Today, notice what comes between you and the happy mind of kindness.

May 2

You won't skid if you stay in a rut.
--Kin Hubbard

Along these lines, Alan Watts wrote a book titled "The Wisdom of Insecurity." One of my favorite quotes is "I don't want to tiptoe through life just to arrive safely at death." (I don't remember who said it.)

ASSIGNMENT: Today, practice finding the part of you that does not value being in a rut, the part that is not afraid to live with joyous abandon.

May 3

I expect to pass through this life but once.
If therefore there be any kindness I can
show, or any good thing I can do for any
fellow being, let me do it now, as I shall not
pass this way again.
--William Penn

ASSIGNMENT: Today, look to see what "good
things" you want to do while you still have
time.

May 4

Happiness is when what you think, what you say, and what you do are in harmony.
--Mahatma Gandhi

ASSIGNMENT: Today, consider if there is disharmony, where it exists, whether in thinking, speaking, or acting.

May 5

I believe that we are solely responsible for our choices, and we have to accept the consequences of every deed, word, and thought throughout our lifetime.
--Elisabeth Kubler-Ross

ASSIGNMENT: Today, notice how your thoughts have consequences, even if you don't express or act on them.

May 6

And we should consider every day lost on which we have not danced at least once. And we should call every truth false which was not accompanied by at least one laugh.
--Friedrich Nietzsche

ASSIGNMENT: Today, dance at least once and laugh with at least one "truth."

I don't know what your destiny will be, but one thing I do know: the only ones among you who will be really happy are those who have sought and found how to serve.
--Albert Schweitzer

Many of us are taught to approach service with fear and dread. Service is being required to do what you don't want to do because it's the right thing to do and you should do it. What if that's not true at all?

ASSIGNMENT: Today, look to see what you would serve with joy.

May 8

Happiness often sneaks in through a door you didn't know you left open.
--John Barrymore

ASSIGNMENT: Today, leave a few doors open for happiness. Leave them open intentionally!

May 9

Science is organized knowledge. Wisdom is organized life.
--Immanuel Kant

ASSIGNMENT: Today, see how your growing wisdom "organizes" life.

May 10

Life begets life. Energy becomes energy. It is by spending oneself that one becomes rich.
--Sarah Bernhardt

What a joy to throw oneself into something one loves with wild abandon.

ASSIGNMENT: Today, find something to spend yourself on that makes you rich with life's energy.

May 11

Half our life is spent trying to find
something to do with the time we have
rushed through life trying to save.
--Will Rogers

ASSIGNMENT: Today, each time you find
yourself rushing to save time, stop, take a
long deep breath, notice where you are, and
say "thank you."

May 12

The sun, with all those planets revolving around it and dependent upon it, can still ripen a bunch of grapes as if it had nothing else in the universe to do.
--Galileo

ASSIGNMENT: Today, using the sun as your role model, give yourself three of those "nothing else in the universe to do" moments.

A friend once inquired if Gandhi's aim in settling in the village and serving the villagers as best he could was purely humanitarian. Gandhi replied, "I am here to serve no one else but myself, to find my own self-realization through the service of these village folk."

ASSIGNMENT: Today, look to see how you would view service if you truly realized all service is for your own self-realization and freedom.

May 14

All the beautiful sentiments in the world
weigh less than a single lovely action.
--James Russell Lowell

ASSIGNMENT: Today, give yourself a "single
lovely action." Keep in mind that it doesn't
say *big* single lovely action.

May 15

Love the animals, love the plants, love everything. If you love everything, you will perceive the divine mystery in things. Once you perceive it, you will begin to comprehend it better every day. And you will come at last to love the whole world with an all-embracing love.
--Fyodor Dostoyevsky

ASSIGNMENT: Today, pick just one thing to love with full conscious awareness. Hint: That one thing could be you.

May 16

This is the true joy of Life, the being used for a purpose recognized by yourself as a mighty one... the being a force of Nature instead of a feverish, selfish little clod of ailments and grievances complaining that the world will not devote itself to making you happy.
--George Bernard Shaw

ASSIGNMENT: Today, consider what mighty purpose you could give yourself to. (Any voices telling you such a thing is not possible are not part of today's focus!)

May 17

Happiness is as a butterfly which, when pursued, is always beyond our grasp, but which if you will sit down quietly, may alight upon you.
--Nathaniel Hawthorne

ASSIGNMENT: Today, give yourself a few moments to sit down quietly and allow the butterfly of happiness to alight upon you.

May 18

If you see no reason for giving thanks, the fault lies in yourself.
--American Indian proverb

ASSIGNMENT: Today, make a list of ten things you are thankful for.

May 19

Give what you have. To someone, it may be better than you dare to think.
--Henry Wadsworth Longfellow

ASSIGNMENT: Today, give something, anything, with all your heart.

May 20

It is in playing safe that we create a world
of utmost insecurity.
--Dag Hammarskjld

ASSIGNMENT: Today, look at some of the
ways playing safe makes you feel insecure.

Not to hurt our humble brethren (the animals) is our first duty to them, but to stop there is not enough. We have a higher mission: to be of service to them whenever they require it. If you have people who will exclude any of God's creatures from the shelter of compassion and pity, you will have people who will deal likewise with their fellow humans.

--St. Francis of Assisi

ASSIGNMENT: Today, notice how you have been conditioned to exclude you, one of God's creatures, from the shelter of compassion and pity.

May 22

The remarkable thing is that we really do love our neighbor as ourselves. We do unto others as we do unto ourselves. We hate others when we hate ourselves. We are tolerant toward others when we tolerate ourselves. We forgive others when we forgive ourselves.
--Eric Hoffer

ASSIGNMENT: Today, consider how love, tolerance, and forgiveness for yourself would change your relationship with the world.

May 23

I learned long ago that those who are the happiest are those who do the most for others.
--Booker T. Washington

ASSIGNMENT: Today, look to see what gets between you and that happiness.

May 24

Love is not a matter of getting what you want. Quite the contrary. The insistence on always having what you want, on always being satisfied, on always being fulfilled, makes love impossible.
--Thomas Merton

ASSIGNMENT: Today, find the moments in which you can trade getting what you want, being satisfied and fulfilled, for love. Notice how that feels.

May 25

The deepest craving of human nature is the need to be appreciated.
--William James

ASSIGNMENT: Today, find as many things as you can to appreciate and appreciate them. Make a list. Keep notes. Read over your list and notes at the end of the day. Be sure you are on the list!

May 26

Self-love is not so vile a sin as self-neglecting.
--William Shakespeare

We are conditioned that love for the self is wrong, selfish, indulgent, and egocentric, which it is when it comes from the ego.

ASSIGNMENT: Today, notice how self-neglecting is as selfish and indulgent as the most egocentric self-love.

Perhaps the most important thing we can undertake toward the reduction of fear is to make it easier for people to accept themselves, to like themselves.
--Bonaro W. Overstreet

ASSIGNMENT: Today, observe the relationship between self-judgment and fear.

May 28

Just because everything is different doesn't mean that everything has changed.
--Irene Peter

ASSIGNMENT: Today, ponder that koan! *
*Koan: a spiritual puzzle that cannot be solved intellectually but must be comprehended in a flash of intuitive knowing.

May 29

Things do not change, we change.
--Henry David Thoreau

ASSIGNMENT: Today, consider how your
changes have resulted in a changed
perception of things.

May 30

The most successful people are those who
are good at plan B.
--James Yorke

ASSIGNMENT: Today, write down the plan B
you currently have - perhaps it has been
unacknowledged - and write down the plan B
you would like to have.

May 31

The more sympathy you give, the less you need.
--Malcolm S. Forbes

ASSIGNMENT: Today, look to see where your sympathy is and where it goes.

June 1

I would rather feel compassion than know
the meaning of it.
--Thomas Aquinas

ASSIGNMENT: Today, explore how
compassion feels to you.

June 2

How far you go in life depends on your being tender with the young, compassionate with the aged, sympathetic with the striving and tolerant of the weak and strong. Because someday in life you will have been all of these.

--George Washington Carver

ASSIGNMENT: Today, take a quiet walk to a lovely spot, sit down and consider the truth of that statement. On the walk back, practice being tender, compassionate, and sympathetic with you.

June 3

The most important things in life are to work and to love.
--Nora Zeal Hurston

ASSIGNMENT: Today, see if you agree with that statement. Look for ways in which your life is in alignment with what is most important to you.

June 4

Happiness comes when your work and words
are of benefit to yourself and others.
--The Buddha

ASSIGNMENT: Today, recall times in your
life when your work and words benefited you
and others.

June 5

Happiness is a thing to be practiced, like the violin.
--John Lubbock

Throughout your life you have practiced many things until they became second nature, even if you don't play a musical instrument, a sport, or participate in some other skilled activity.

ASSIGNMENT: Today, notice when you experience something other than happiness and peace, and practice turning your attention back to that happiness and peace.

June 6

That is happiness: to be dissolved into
something completely great.
--Willa Cather

ASSIGNMENT: Today, consider what that
"completely great" would be for you.

June 7

Appreciation can make a day, even change a
life. Your willingness to put it into words is
all that is necessary.
--Margaret Cousins

ASSIGNMENT: Today, express, in words, an
appreciation.

June 8

The disappearance of a sense of responsibility is the most far-reaching consequence of submission to authority.
--Stanley Milgram

ASSIGNMENT: Today, notice the voices in your head that speak as "authorities." Notice how unquestioningly following those voices relieves you of responsibility for being present.

June 9

When I was young, I used to admire
intelligent people; as I grow older, I admire
kind people.
--Abraham Joshua Heschel

ASSIGNMENT: Today, notice the kind people
you encounter.

No one has ever become poor by giving.
--Anne Frank

ASSIGNMENT: Today, consider what you
believe about giving and about being poor.

June 11

Do all the good you can, by all the means you can, in all the ways you can, in all the places you can, at all the times you can, to all the people you can, as long as ever you can.
--John Wesley

ASSIGNMENT: Today, devote yourself to doing all the good you can.

June 12

One who wishes to secure the good of others has already secured one's own.
--Confucius

Many of us have been taught that it is more blessed to give than to receive; but as Bernard Gunther pointed out, it is more blessed to give *and* receive. Christmas Humphreys said that we are punished *by* what we do, not because of it. The reverse is also true; we are rewarded *by* what we do, not because of it.

ASSIGNMENT: Today, look to see how that has been true in your life.

June 13

Do not go where the path may lead, go instead where there is no path and leave a trail.
--Ralph Waldo Emerson

ASSIGNMENT: Today, consider where you would like to blaze a trail in your life.

June 14

Error is just as important a condition of life
as truth.
--Carl Jung

ASSIGNMENT: Today, appreciate some of
the "errors" in your life that have lead to
"truth."

June 15

The most wasted of all days is one without laughter.

--e.e. cummings

ASSIGNMENT: Today, look for laughter.

June 16

Few are those who see with their own eyes
and feel with their own hearts.
--Albert Einstein

ASSIGNMENT: Today, go beyond belief,
assumption, and conditioning to find *your*
experience.

June 17

To go against the dominant thinking of your friends, of most of the people you see every day, is perhaps the most difficult act of heroism you can perform.
--Theodore H. White

The majority of us find going against accepted mores immensely uncomfortable, even if we secretly believe they are harmful.

ASSIGNMENT: Today, to the extent that you are willing, be a hero and feel what it's like to buck the system.

June 18

Fear grows in darkness; if you think there's a bogeyman around, turn on the light.
--Dorothy Thompson

ASSIGNMENT: Today, through the power of awareness and attention, banish the darkness; turn the light on; keep it on; do not turn it off. If it seems occasionally to go off by itself, watch closely how that happens.

June 19

Not what the eye sees, but that which
makes the eye see, that is the Spirit.
--The Upanishads

ASSIGNMENT: Today, look for the "spirit"
behind *everything*.

June 20

I know what the greatest cure is: it is to
give up, to relinquish, to surrender, so that
our little hearts may beat in unison with the
great heart of the world.
--Henry Miller

ASSIGNMENT: Today, practice saying "yes"
to life with every breath.

June 21

Only when we are no longer afraid do we
begin to live.
--Dorothy Thompson

ASSIGNMENT: Today, in every moment,
imagine your life without fear.

June 22

The world is too dangerous for anything but truth and too small for anything but love.
--William Sloane Coffin

Ram Dass used to talk about life being so scary it made no sense not to hold hands as we go through it.

ASSIGNMENT: Today, in your heart, hold hands with everyone you meet.

June 23

I am always doing that which I cannot do, in order that I may learn how to do it.
--Pablo Picasso

What do you not know how to do that you can do in order to learn how to do it?

ASSIGNMENT: Today, make a curriculum, a lesson plan, for your learning.

June 24

The greatest prayer is patience.
--The Buddha

ASSIGNMENT: Today, be very patient with yourself.

June 25

Be not angry that you cannot make others as you wish them to be, since you cannot make yourself as you wish to be.
--Thomas a Kempis

My mother had this quote taped to the inside of a kitchen cabinet door, and I grew up reading it every time I reached for a clean glass. It has deeply informed my life.

ASSIGNMENT: Today, practice accepting yourself exactly as you are.

June 26

"I see nobody on the road," said Alice.
"I only wish I had such eyes," the King
remarked in a fretful tone. "To be able to
see Nobody! And at that distance too!"
--Lewis Carroll

ASSIGNMENT: Today, enjoy silliness!

June 27

If I had influence with the good fairy who is supposed to preside over the christening of all children, I should ask that her gift to each child in the world be a sense of wonder so indestructible that it would last throughout life.
--Rachel Carson

ASSIGNMENT: Today, revive your sense of wonder.

June 28

Think of Zen, of the Void, of Good and Evil, and you are bound hand and foot. Think only and entirely and completely of what you are doing in the moment and you are free as a bird.
--R. H. Blyth

ASSIGNMENT: Today, find three activities with which you will practice thinking only, entirely, and completely of what you are doing in the moment.

June 29

You are the sum total of everything it has
taken to produce you since before the
beginning of beginningless time.
--Buddhist saying

ASSIGNMENT: Today, honor such a
magnificent being - you!

June 30

I embrace emerging experience. I participate in discovery.
I am a butterfly. I am not a butterfly collector.
--William Stafford

ASSIGNMENT: Today, practice being the butterfly of happiness

July 1

To say yes, you have to sweat and roll up your sleeves, and plunge both hands into life up to the elbows. It is easy to say no, even if saying no means death.
--Jean Anouilh

ASSIGNMENT: Today, look for those moments in which you can trade no for yes.

July 2

I imagine that yes is the only living thing.
--e.e. cummings

ASSIGNMENT: Today, feel the power in a
wholehearted "yes!"

July 3

I neglect God and his Angels, for the noise
of a fly, for the rattling of a coach, for the
whining of a door.
--John Donne

ASSIGNMENT: Today, notice which of life's
little irritations you give up your peace and
joy for.

July 4

I have now reigned about 50 years in victory or peace, beloved by my subjects, dreaded by my enemies, and respected by my allies. Riches and honors, power and pleasure, have waited on my call... In this situation, I have diligently numbered the days of pure and genuine happiness which have fallen to my lot. They amount to fourteen.
--Abd Er-Rahman III of Spain (960 C.E.)

Conditioning works hard to make us believe the lie that if the externals of life were different we would be happy and satisfied.

ASSIGNMENT: Today, take responsibility for your "pure and genuine happiness." Find it inside and enjoy it.

July 5

The greatest part of our happiness depends on our dispositions, not our circumstances.
--Martha Washington

ASSIGNMENT: Today, notice how you have been conditioned to let externals determine your happiness, and find the place inside where true happiness resides.

July 6

Just remain in the center watching. Then
forget that you are there.
--Lao-Tzu

ASSIGNMENT: Today, as often as you can
remember, give all your attention and
awareness to all that surrounds and reflects
you.

July 7

The range of what we think and do is limited by what we fail to notice. And because we fail to notice that we fail to notice, there is little we can do to change until we notice how failing to notice shapes our thoughts and deeds.

--R. D. Laing

ASSIGNMENT: Today, notice! Notice what? Notice everything you can, especially what you have previously failed to notice.

July 8

You and I are all as much continuous with the physical universe as a wave is continuous with the ocean. You are a function of this total galaxy, bounded by the Milky Way, and this galaxy is a function of all other galaxies. You are that vast thing that you see far, far off with great telescopes. You are the eternal thing that comes and goes that appears - now as John Jones, now as Mary Smith, now as Betty Brown - and so it goes, forever and ever and ever.
--Alan Watts

ASSIGNMENT: Today, *feel* yourself in that interconnected reality. Hint: It can be helpful to find a quiet, secluded place to practice this.

July 9

The reason we want to go on and on is because we live in an impoverished present.
 --Alan Watts

ASSIGNMENT: Today, consider how you want to *be*.

July 10

It is no use walking anywhere to preach
unless our walking is our preaching.
--St. Francis of Assisi

Or as one of our book titles puts it: How
You Do Anything Is How You Do Everything.

ASSIGNMENT: Today, see what you are
"preaching" as you walk.

July 11

In about the same degree as you are
helpful, you will be happy.
--Karl Reiland

ASSIGNMENT: Today, do something genuinely
helpful for you.

July 12

Too many people are thinking of security instead of opportunity. They seem to be more afraid of life than death
--James F. Bymes

ASSIGNMENT: Today, consider if how you live your life indicates a greater fear of death or of life.

July 13

None are so old as those who have outlived
enthusiasm.
--Henry David Thoreau

ASSIGNMENT: Today, keep company with the
enthusiastic youngster inside.

July 14

Don't be afraid to go out on a limb. That's where the fruit is.
--H. Jackson Browne

ASSIGNMENT: Today, go out on a limb for something. Pick something sweet.

July 15

The entire world is a mirror. The only thing
you can ever experience is yourself.
Everything you think, feel, do, and see is you.
Your thoughts, feelings, ideas, values,
philosophies, and opinions create your world.
Everything you experience is as it is because
that's how you experience it. We experience
the world the way we do because of who we
are, not because of how it is.
--from *The Key and the Name of the Key*
Is Willingness

ASSIGNMENT: Today, without allowing the
voices of conditioning any opinions at all,
allow yourself to see yourself through the
world you are projecting.

July 16

The world is a looking glass and gives back to each of us the reflection of our own face.
--William Makepeace Thackeray

ASSIGNMENT: Today, see yourself reflected in all that surrounds you.

July 17

None are so hopelessly enslaved as those
who falsely believe they are free.
--Goethe

ASSIGNMENT: Today, consider how the
limitations of what you have been conditioned
to believe keep you from seeing what is so
and what is possible.

If a pickpocket meets a holy man, he will
see only his pockets.
--Hari Dass

ASSIGNMENT: Today, see the beauty around
you and know you are projecting that beauty.

July 19

The same eyes with which I see God, God
sees me.
--Meister Eckhart

ASSIGNMENT: Today, consider that you are,
perhaps, "created in God's image," but
surely "God" is created in your image.

July 20

Two Zen masters were walking beside a stream.

"How happily the fish are swimming in the stream," observed one.

"You do not know the fish are swimming happily," observed the other, thoroughly schooled in the notion of projection!

"You do not know that I do not know that the fish are swimming happily," countered the first, apparently even more thoroughly schooled in the notion of projection!

--old Zen story

ASSIGNMENT: Do the voices of conditioning encourage you to see projection as something wrong? Today, can you use your projections to see *you* more clearly?

July 21

If you want to understand what a
watermelon is, you take a watermelon, get a
knife, and cut the watermelon. Then you put
a slice in your mouth. Boom! YOUR
experience!
--Seung Sahn

ASSIGNMENT: Today, in at least one
situation you're conditioned to assume about
rather than being present to, refuse. Have
your own experience instead.

July 22

Concert pianist Vladimir Horowitz tells about the time he played a dissonant contemporary composition at a private gathering. When he finished, someone asked, "I don't understand what that composition means, Mr. Horowitz. Could you please explain it?" Without a word, Horowitz played the composition again. When he finished he turned to his questioner and said, "That's what it means."

Conditioned mind is always arguing for meaning precisely because there is no such thing, and the way to stay busy is to try to find something that doesn't exist.

ASSIGNMENT: Today, have a meaningless day--and enjoy every minute of it!

July 23

I learn by going where I have to go.
--Theodore Roethke

ASSIGNMENT: Today, let life lead you and remind yourself that going where life leads you is life's gift to you.

July 24

Zen means doing ordinary things willingly and cheerfully.
--R.H. Blyth

Of course Zen doesn't "mean" anything. But we can still do ordinary things willingly and cheerfully.

ASSIGNMENT: Today, do what you do with willingness and cheer and prove to yourself that there are no "ordinary" things.

July 25

Do or do not. There is no try.
--Yoda, *The Empire Strikes Back*

ASSIGNMENT: Today, do be the person you
want to be as often as you remember to.

July 26

I respectfully decline the invitation to join your hallucination.
--Scott Adams

Supposedly, the Buddha said 2500 years ago, "Society is insane." It appears not much has changed!

ASSIGNMENT: Today, identify an aspect of society that is, for you, insane and hallucinatory and respectfully decline to participate in it.

July 27

With every gust of wind,
the butterfly changes its place
on the willow.
--Basho

ASSIGNMENT: Today, be flexible!

I do not understand Buddhism.
--Hui Neng (Sixth Patriarch of Zen)

We cannot understand Buddhism or anything
else because there is nothing to understand
and no one to understand it.

ASSIGNMENT: Today, enjoy being a person
of no understanding.

July 29

If you are distressed by anything external, the pain is not due to the thing itself, but to your estimate of it; and this you have the power to revoke at any moment.
--Marcus Aurelius

The Buddha taught that we suffer because we cling. "Clinging" is defined as "holding on or pushing away," which are the same thing. Both require intense focus and energy.

ASSIGNMENT: Today, notice how "your estimate" of a thing determines your experience of it. If your experience is suffering, revoke your estimate.

July 30

Dream as if you'll live forever. Live as if you'll die today.
--James Dean

ASSIGNMENT: What is a dream you have that is remaining unfulfilled for no good reason?

July 31

Cats seem to go on the principle that it never does any harm to ask for what you want.
--Joseph Wood Krutch

ASSIGNMENT: Today, ask for what you want for the practice of asking, just to see what happens, not because you have an expectation that you will get what you ask for.

August 1

Start by doing what's necessary; then do what's possible; and suddenly you are doing the impossible.
--St. Francis of Assisi

ASSIGNMENT: Today, bring enjoyment to doing what is necessary and allow that enjoyment to open you to what is possible.

August 2

Tell me to what you pay attention and I will
tell you who you are.
--Jose Ortega y Gasset

ASSIGNMENT: Today, without judgment or
self-hatred, look to see what your habitual
focus of attention says about who you are.

August 3

One of the nice things about problems is
that a good many of them do not exist
except in our imaginations.
--Steve Allen

ASSIGNMENT: Today, notice how conditioned
mind creates problems. Ask yourself, "If I
didn't experience this as a problem, would it
be one?"

August 4

One doesn't discover new lands without consenting to lose sight of the shore for a very long time.
--Andre Gide

To take in that quote one must "lose sight of the shore," if only briefly. That shift in attention is all that is required to open the doorway to infinite lands of discovery.

ASSIGNMENT: Today, practice that shift in attention from conditioned mind to *here*.

August 5

If you're going through hell, keep going.
--Winston Churchill

ASSIGNMENT: Today, whatever you're going
through, keep going - and smile!

August 6

Every moment is a golden one for those who have the vision to recognize it as such.
--Henry Miller

ASSIGNMENT: Today, be a person of golden moments.

August 7

People think love is an emotion. Love is good sense.
--Ken Kesey

ASSIGNMENT: Today, appreciate your good sense!

August 8

The greatest thing you'll ever learn is just to love and be loved in return.
--Eden Ahbez, "Nature Boy" (song, recorded by Nat King Cole)

ASSIGNMENT: Today, learn to your heart's content.

August 9

It is a great obstacle to happiness to expect too much.
--Bernard de Fontenelle

ASSIGNMENT: Today, lower your expectations and enjoy the happiness of being with what is.

August 10

There isn't any secret formula or method.
You learn love by loving, by paying attention
and doing what one thereby discovers has to
be done.
--Aldous Huxley

ASSIGNMENT: Today, consider what you're
committed to and remind yourself that you
are paying attention, that you are learning
to love by loving what you're committed to.

August 11

Am I not destroying my enemies when I make friends of them?
--Abraham Lincoln

ASSIGNMENT: Today, every time you hear a self-hating comment go through your head, blithely, smilingly, yet unbelievingly, agree with it. ("Did you just say I'm selfish? Well, yes, you're right, sometimes I am.")

August 12

Be observant if you would have a pure
heart, for something is born to you in
consequence of every action.
--Jelaluddin Rumi

ASSIGNMENT: Today, know that you "would
have a pure heart," that in fact you already
have a pure heart, and you are doing all you
can to live from that pure heart each
moment.

August 13

Anything that is given can be at once taken away. We have to learn never to expect anything, and when something comes it's no more than a gift on loan.
--John McGahern

ASSIGNMENT: Today, enjoy the many gifts you've been loaned.

August 14

No snowflake in an avalanche ever feels responsible.
-- Francois-Marie Voltaire

ASSIGNMENT: Today, notice whether there are aspects of your life that you go along with without thought - maybe out of habit - and, just for today, take responsibility and refuse to participate.

August 15

Freedom of will is the ability to do gladly
what which I must do.
--C. J. Jung

ASSIGNMENT: Today, let yourself do gladly
what you "must" do.

August 16

To know what you prefer instead of humbly saying Amen to what the world tells you you ought to prefer, is to have kept your soul alive.
--Robert Louis Stevenson

There is a vast difference between "the world" and "life."

ASSIGNMENT: Today, let yourself prefer life; be in the world, but not of it.

August 17

For everything that lives is holy, life delights
in life.
--William Blake

ASSIGNMENT: Today, delight in life delighting
in life.

August 18

Take away love and our earth is a tomb.
--Robert Browning

ASSIGNMENT: Today, feel the love that
makes life worth living. Hint: That love *is* life
living.

August 19

What lies behind us and what lies before us
are small matters compared to what lies
within us.
--Oliver Wendell Holmes

ASSIGNMENT: Today, spend some present,
conscious time with that which lies within you.

August 20

You can't make a place for yourself in the sun if you keep taking refuge under the family tree.
--Helen Keller

ASSIGNMENT: Today, see yourself without needing to reference where you've come from or who influenced you. Appreciate the you that you are today, standing on your own.

August 21

The hardest arithmetic to master is that
which enables us to count our blessings.
--Eric Hoffer

ASSIGNMENT: Today, start counting!

August 22

I want a busy life, a just mind, and a timely death.
--Zora Neale Hurston

ASSIGNMENT: Today, consider what you want for your life and write it on a poster.

August 23

"I have done my best."
That is about all the philosophy of living that one needs.
--Lin-Yutang

Conditioning will try to convince us that we've never done our best, that we should have done better, should have known better, and that to claim otherwise is a lie.

ASSIGNMENT: Today, admit to yourself that you have always done your best.

August 24

Loneliness is the poverty of self; solitude is the richness of self.
--May Sarton

Many of us have been conditioned to find being alone with the self frightening or unpleasant. This is often because in quiet and a lack of distraction the voices in our heads are loud, distressing, and unavoidable. As we learn to appreciate and enjoy who we truly are, rather than fearing the person the voices project we are, we begin to crave alone time with that person we love.

ASSIGNMENT: Today, give yourself some solitude.

August 25

Nature abhors a vacuum, and if I can only walk with sufficient carelessness I am sure to be filled.
--Henry David Thoreau

ASSIGNMENT: Today, give yourself some time in nature and let it fill you. As you walk, breathe into your heart all the green around you.

August 26

And the trouble is, if you don't risk
anything, you risk even more.
--Erica Jong

As the old joke states, no one on their
death bed ever said, "I wish I'd spent more
time in the office."

ASSIGNMENT: Today, just for a while, risk
having the life you want.

August 27

The failure is wonderful indeed!
--Mumon

ASSIGNMENT: Today, stop for just a
moment and picture the freedom and joy
that accompany viewing failure as something
wonderful. Feel that several times during
today.

August 28

Mistakes are the portals of discovery.
--James Joyce

We can't learn anything new while focused on what we think we know.

ASSIGNMENT: Today, notice the portal of discovery in at least one "mistake." Hint: You won't see it if you're focusing on the voices telling you what you did wrong.

August 29

If you want a guarantee, buy a toaster.
--Clint Eastwood

ASSIGNMENT: Today, notice how you confuse expectation and assumption with what is and become upset if life isn't the way you think it should be.

August 30

I'm a great believer in luck and I find the harder I work, the more I have of it.
--Thomas Jefferson

Conditioning would have us believe that everything should be easy. We shouldn't have to try hard or work hard or even show up with enthusiasm, sincerity, or willingness. The voices will simultaneously tell us that we're worthless and deserve everything.

ASSIGNMENT: Today, see if you're willing to work hard to be "lucky."

August 31

Opportunity is missed by most because it is dressed in overalls and looks like work.
--Thomas Alva Edison

ASSIGNMENT: Today, consider that working hard and playing hard are the same thing when we're living from the heart.

September 1

A rut is a grave with the ends knocked out.
--Laurence J. Peter

ASSIGNMENT: Today, spend at least an hour the way you'd like to spend eternity.

September 2

To be surprised, to wonder, is to begin to understand.
--Jose Ortega y Gasset

Conditioned mind, or karma, is the only thing that wants to be right and thinks it is. We can't know anything about life except what has already happened. (And that's all projection!) What we habitually *think* is conditioning.

ASSIGNMENT: Today, get out of your head and let life surprise you.

September 3

Pai Lo-tien, a Chinese poet, asked a Zen master,
"What is Buddha's teaching?"
The master said, "Buddha's teaching is to do something good, not do something bad."
Pai Lo-tien said, "That's pretty easy, even a three-year-old knows that."
"Even though a three-year-old knows this, an eighty-year-old doesn't do it," the master replied.
--Zen mondo

ASSIGNMENT: Today, notice how you get talked out of doing the thing you know is good to do.

September 4

It is easier to fight for one's principles than to live up to them.
--Alfred Adler

ASSIGNMENT: Today, consider how hard it is to be a person of principle and let the compassion of that knowledge inspire more tolerance for others and greater effort for yourself.

September 5

Seek not to follow in the footsteps of the wise of old, seek what they sought.
--Matsuo Basho

ASSIGNMENT: Today, give yourself a little time in silence and solitude to commune with wisdom. Not thinking or knowing. Wisdom. (Repeat often!)

September 6

The only people with whom you should try to get even are those who have helped you.
--John Southard

ASSIGNMENT: Today, wreak vengeance!

September 7

Something we were withholding made us weak
Until we found it was ourselves.
--Robert Frost

ASSIGNMENT: Today, see what you are
willing to fully give yourself to. Hint: It
doesn't have to be something big.
Wholeheartedness is a process and a habit.

September 8

The best guide in life is strength. In religion, as in all other matters, discard everything that weakens you, have nothing to do with it. --Swami Vivekananda

ASSIGNMENT: Today, consider one thing that weakens you that you're willing to let go. Hint: Believing the voices would be a good place to start!

September 9

Truth is completely spontaneous. Lies have to be taught.
--Buckminster Fuller

Did you see the truth of that the moment you read it?

ASSIGNMENT: Today, practice not believing the lies conditioned mind is repeating to you.

September 10

Things don't change, but by and by our
wishes change.
--Marcel Proust

ASSIGNMENT: Today, consider some of the
things you wished for in youth that you no
longer wish for.

September 11

The winds of grace blow all the time. All we need to do is set our sails.
--Ramakrishna

ASSIGNMENT: Today, stop often to feel the breezes of grace.

September 12

Today, like every other day, we wake up
empty and frightened. Don't open the door
to the study and begin reading. Take down
the dulcimer. Let the beauty we love be
what we do. There are hundreds of ways to
kneel and kiss the ground.
--Jalaluddin Rumi

ASSIGNMENT: Today, find the willingness to
spend the majority of your day in the
beauty that you love.

September 13

Gratitude!
    Tears melting into
mountain snow
--Soen Nakagawa

ASSIGNMENT: Today, as you go through your day, notice everything for which you are grateful.

September 14

No one has ever loved anyone the way everyone wants to be loved.
--Mignon Mclaughlin

ASSIGNMENT: Today, consider that only each of us can give that love to ourselves and it is from that fulfillment that we love others.

September 15

Let us be kinder to one another.
--Aldous Huxley's last words

ASSIGNMENT: Today, let kindness direct your every movement.

September 16

Think every day your last: you will receive
with joy hours on which you have not
counted.
--Horace

ASSIGNMENT: Today, set aside the
conversation in your mind and live with *life*.

September 17

May you live all the days of your life.
--Jonathan Swift

ASSIGNMENT: Today, practice being fully
alive. Breathe. Feel. See. Hear.

September 18

I live in possibility.
--Emily Dickinson

ASSIGNMENT: Today, be aware of possibility
before the voices talk you into defeat.

September 19

Be like the bird, pausing in its flight
On limb too slight,
Feels it give way, yet sings,
Knowing it has wings.
--Victor Hugo

ASSIGNMENT: Today, spread your wings.
Sing!

September 20

Like all dreamers I confuse disenchantment
with truth.
--Jean-Paul Sartre

ASSIGNMENT: Today, notice how you confuse
the negativity of the voices of conditioning
with truth.

September 21

Each day, death strikes, and we live as though we were immortal. This is the greatest marvel.
--The Mahabharata

One of my favorite reminders is "don't postpone joy."

ASSIGNMENT: Today, notice what you focus on as if you have an eternity to choose-- later-- the life you truly want.

September 22

To the person who is afraid, everything rustles.

--Sophocles

ASSIGNMENT: Today, notice how you feel afraid.

September 23

We fear something before we hate it. A child who fears noises becomes an adult who hates noise.

--Cyril Connolly

ASSIGNMENT: Today, notice the fear behind the things you hate.

September 24

I tell you: one must still have chaos in one,
to give birth to a dancing star.
--Friedrich Nietzsche

ASSIGNMENT: Today, see if you can see the
chaos, the disorder, the incompleteness in
you as steps in your dance with life.

September 25

If I could tell you what it meant, there
would be no point in dancing it.
--Isadora Duncan

Dance has no meaning, music has no
meaning, nature has no meaning, life has no
meaning.

ASSIGNMENT: Today, remind yourself that a
lack of meaning means (!) we can enjoy
everything.

September 26

Your understandings are of
misunderstandings.
--St. Francis of Assisi

ASSIGNMENT: Today, notice how far
conditioned mind's "knowing" and
"understanding" pull you from being *here*
where life happens.

September 27

Do not seek after enlightenment. Simply
cease to cherish opinions.
--Zen saying

Can you sense how much easier life would
be if you didn't have to stumble over your
opinions moment by moment? Opinions add
suffering-producing layers, obscuring what is.

ASSIGNMENT: Today, without judgment,
simply notice your opinions.

September 28

Carpe diem, quam minimum credula postero.
Seize today, and put as little trust as you
can in the morrow.
--Horace

ASSIGNMENT: Today, be and do as if there
will be no tomorrow.

September 29

To describe myself in a scientific way, I must also describe my surroundings, which is a clumsy way of getting around to the realization that you are the entire universe.
--Alan Watts

ASSIGNMENT: Today, explore your connection to all that is. Try to find a line where you begin and end. Hint: "My skin" is not the answer. Keep looking.

September 30

If you wish to make an apple pie from scratch, first you must create the universe.
--Carl Sagan

ASSIGNMENT: Today, continue to explore the oneness that is "us."

October 1

Only barbarians are not curious about where
they come from, how they came to be
where they are, where they appear to be
going, whether they wish to go there, and if
so, why, and if not, why not.
--Isaiah Berlin

ASSIGNMENT: Today, spend a little time
just being *here*. Let the thinking mind go and
be a barbarian!

October 2

One of the saddest lessons of history is this:
If we've been bamboozled long enough, we
tend to reject any evidence of the
bamboozle.
--Carl Sagan

Conditioned people are terrified of being
brainwashed, but that's because conditioning
IS the brainwashing, and it doesn't want
competition.

ASSIGNMENT: Today, watch the thoughts
that come through, the incessant
conversation in the mind, and consider that
it is a pre-programmed tape-loop.

October 3

We cannot see things as they really are until we let go the idea of a separate self.
--John Daido Loori

ASSIGNMENT: Today, practice seeing that you are in life as a fish is in the ocean--at one with, a product of, unable to live without, not separate in any way.

October 4

To feel life is meaningless unless "I" can be permanent is like having desperately fallen in love with an inch.
--Alan Watts

ASSIGNMENT: Today, notice what silliness and suffering result from believing oneself to be an ego that wants to be the most important thing in life.

October 5

People go abroad to wonder at the heights
of mountains, at the huge waves of the sea,
at the long courses of rivers, at the vast
compass of the ocean, at the circular
motions of the stars; and they pass by
themselves without wondering.
--Saint Augustin

ASSIGNMENT: Notice today how wonder
collapses under the weight of meaning.

October 6

Of all the self-fulfilling prophecies in our
culture, the assumption that aging means
decline and poor health is probably the
deadliest.
--Marilyn Ferguson

ASSIGNMENT: Today, question at least one
such deadly self-fulfilling assumption.

October 7

From the very beginning,
all beings are Buddha.
--Zen Master Hakuin

ASSIGNMENT: Today, practice being the
Buddha. How will you *be*?

October 8

A mouse is miracle enough to stagger
sextillions of infidels.
--Walt Whitman

ASSIGNMENT: Today, notice, really *see*, just
a few of the miracles you ordinarily would
ignore.

October 9

The higher the truth, the simpler it is.
--Abraham Isaac Kook

ASSIGNMENT: Today, consider what high truths you are missing because they are so simple.

October 10

We are always paid for our suspicion by finding what we suspect.
--Henry David Thoreau

One great seer after another tells us this same basic message: we see what we expect to see.

ASSIGNMENT: Today, watch this process within you - no judgment, please.

October 11

There is no reality except the one contained within us. That is why so many people live such an unreal life. They take the images outside them for reality and never let the world within assert itself.
--Hermann Hesse

ASSIGNMENT: Today, let "the world within" have the day.

October 12

Reality is that which, when you stop believing in it, doesn't go away.
--Philip K. Dick

ASSIGNMENT: Today, spend a little time with that which does not need to be maintained. Hint: Notice that the voices in your head need constant attention in order to appear real.

October 13

Nirvana is right here, before our eyes.
--Zen Master Hakuin

There is no tomorrow, no alternative reality, nothing to look forward to. This is it. This, here, now, is nirvana.

ASSIGNMENT: Today, take a deep breath and let yourself enjoy *this*.

October 14

In this twentieth century, to stop rushing around, to sit quietly on the grass, to switch off the world and come back to the earth, to allow the eye to see a willow, a bush, a cloud, a leaf, is an unforgettable experience.
--Frederick Franck

ASSIGNMENT: Today, give yourself that unforgettable experience.

October 15

While working, while eating, while playing, while walking and while driving, always keep the question, "What am I?"
--Seung Sahn

ASSIGNMENT: Today, as you go through your day, stay in the question "what am I?" This is a good time to tie a string around your finger to aid in remembering to ask that question.

October 16

When you eventually see through the veils
to how things really are, you will keep saying
again and again, "This is certainly not like we
thought it was."
--Jalaluddin Rumi

ASSIGNMENT: Today, allow some gaps in the
thinking so you can see through the veils.

October 17

Those who seek the easy way do not seek the true way.
--Dogen

Life is hard and then you realize it isn't.

ASSIGNMENT: Today, drop the chatter, take a breath, and enjoy the ease.

October 18

A billion stars go spinning
through the night,
blazing high above your head.
But IN you is the presence that will be,
when the stars are dead.
--Rainer Maria Rilke

ASSIGNMENT: Today, take some "time-out"
to be with that presence.

October 19

All conditioned things are impermanent.
Work out your own salvation with diligence.
--The Buddha's last words

ASSIGNMENT: Today, realize that part of
working out one's salvation is to give up the
notion that there is a someone who needs
to be saved.

October 20

The moment is the sole reality.
--Karl Jaspers

ASSIGNMENT: Today, let go the distraction
long enough to sense reality⟹here, now,
this.

October 21

And if there is not any such thing as a long time, nor the rest of your lives, nor from now on, but there is only now, why then now is the thing to praise and I am very happy with it.
--Ernest Hemingway

ASSIGNMENT: Today, find some moments to be happy with what is now.

October 22

Do you think I know what I'm doing?
That for one breath or half-breath
I belong to myself?
As much as a pen knows what it's writing,
or the ball can guess where it's going next.
--Jelaluddin Rumi

ASSIGNMENT: Today, practice letting go and
letting life live you.

October 23

A person can learn nothing except by going
from the known to the unknown.
--Claude Bernard

ASSIGNMENT: Today, release your grasp on
what you think you know and slip in to the
ease of not knowing.

October 24

If you think that you know much, you know little.

--The Upanishads

ASSIGNMENT: Today, can you see how "knowing" prevents "being"?

October 25

The only things worth learning are the things
you learn after you know it all.
--Harry Truman

ASSIGNMENT: Today, be like a child, joyful in
discovering a new world you know nothing
about.

October 26

One must let the play happen to one; one must let the mind loose to respond as it will, to receive impressions, to sense rather than know, to gather rather than immediately understand.
--Edward Albee

You were most likely taught as a child to try to understand and make sense of experience so that you could feel safe and in control.

ASSIGNMENT: Today, see life as a play and simply "gather rather than immediately understand."

October 27

All the troubles of humanity come from not knowing how to sit still.
--Blaise Pascal

ASSIGNMENT: Today, sit down, sit still, and appreciate the person willing to sit still with life as it is.

October 28

It's never too late to do nothing.
--Zen saying

ASSIGNMENT: Today, spend at least a little time doing nothing but being.

October 29

There's nothing in this world I dislike.
--Zen Master Rinzai

ASSIGNMENT: Today, notice how liking and disliking destroys the ability to enjoy.

October 30

For every minute you are angry, you lose sixty seconds of happiness.
--Ralph Waldo Emerson

ASSIGNMENT: Today, practice dropping upset, turning the attention away from the conditioned conversation in the head and to the happiness of *here*.

October 31

Never be ashamed to admit you are in the wrong---it's just another way to say you are wiser today than yesterday.
--Jonathan Swift

ASSIGNMENT: Today, notice how often you can be wiser than you were the moment before!

November 1

Success is going from failure to failure
without losing enthusiasm.
--Winston Churchill

ASSIGNMENT: Today, make a list of failures
that, in retrospect, helped you on your way.

November 2

Nothing in life is to be feared. It is only to
be understood.
--Marie Curie

ASSIGNMENT: Today, choose a fear and
embrace it in conscious, compassionate
awareness.

November 3

Greed is so well organized that we call it economic prosperity.
Ill will is so organized that we call it defense and we make weapons and war.
Ignorance is so well organized that we study about everything except ourselves.
I try to decrease the thoughts in my mind.
If we stopped thinking we'd have no problems.
--Ari Yaratne (called the Gandhi of Sri Lanka)

ASSIGNMENT: Today, consider how many problems you would have if the conditioned conversations in your mind were to stop.

November 4

"I have done that," says my memory. "I cannot have done that," says my pride, and remains adamant. At last, memory yields.
--Nietzsche

This is such a perfect expression of the way conditioned mind does what it does.

ASSIGNMENT: Today, watch how conditioned mind wages its constant campaigns to convince you that what is not true is true.

November 5

The intelligent man who is proud of his
intelligence is like the condemned man who is
proud of his large cell.
--Simone Weil

ASSIGNMENT: Today, consider the
difference between knowledge and wisdom.

November 6

"I can't believe that," said Alice.
"Can't you?" the Queen said, in a pitying
tone. "Try again: draw a long breath and
shut your eyes."
Alice laughed. "There's no use trying," she
said. "One can't believe impossible things."
"I dare say you haven't had much practice,"
said the Queen. "When I was younger, I
always did it for half an hour a day. Why
sometimes I've believed as many as six
impossible things before breakfast."
--Lewis Carroll

ASSIGNMENT: Today, consider how many
impossibly absurd things you've been
conditioned to believe.

November 7

Most human beings have an almost infinite
capacity for taking things for granted.
--Aldous Huxley

ASSIGNMENT: Today, just notice the things
you take for granted. Make a list. Say
"thank you" for each of them.

November 8

Courage is the price that life exacts for
granting peace.
--Amelia Earhart

ASSIGNMENT: Today, find the courage to
let go conditioned mind for a few moments
and feel the peace of its absence.

November 9

There is no cure for birth and death save
to enjoy the interval.
--George Santayana

ASSIGNMENT: Today, as often as you
remember: enjoy the interval.

November 10

Your task is not to seek for love, but
merely to seek and find all the barriers
within yourself that you have built against it.
--Jelaluddin Rumi

ASSIGNMENT: Today, notice three of those
barriers against love.

November 11

Criticism is prejudice made plausible.
--H. L. Mencken

ASSIGNMENT: Today, focus your attention
on criticism, and when you find it, drop it
and return to the breath.

November 12

Constant kindness can accomplish much. As the sun makes ice melt, kindness causes misunderstanding, mistrust, and hostility to evaporate.
--Albert Schweitzer

ASSIGNMENT: Today, melt with kindness.

November 13

We read the world wrong and say that it deceives us.
--Rabindranath Tagore

ASSIGNMENT: Today, notice how often your disappointments are the result of false assumptions.

November 14

Paradise is where I am.
--Voltaire

ASSIGNMENT: Today, look around, take a breath, be *here*, and notice that you are in paradise.

November 15

There is no duty we so underrate as the
duty of being happy. By being happy we sow
anonymous benefits upon the world.
--Robert Louis Stevenson

ASSIGNMENT: Today, are you willing to do
your duty?

November 16

Expecting the world to treat you fairly because you are a good person is a little like expecting the bull not to attack you because you are a vegetarian.
--Dennis Wholey

ASSIGNMENT: Today, treat the world fairly.

November 17

Reexamine all that you have been told in school, or in church or in any book. Dismiss whatever insults your soul.
--Walt Whitman

ASSIGNMENT: Today, as you dismiss the conditioning that "insults your soul," replace it with that which uplifts your soul.

November 18

Friendship with oneself is all important because without it one cannot be friends with anybody else in the world.
--Eleanor Roosevelt

ASSIGNMENT: Today, pay particular attention to the voices that speak to you disrespectfully.

November 19

The greatest work that kindness does to others is that it makes them kind themselves.
--Amelia Earhart

ASSIGNMENT: Today, declare this day as "Kindness Day," and interact accordingly.

November 20

Bite off more than you can chew, then chew it.
--Ella Williams

ASSIGNMENT: Remind yourself that you are equal to your life, no matter how big your life gets!

November 21

A person who is nice to you but rude to the waiter is not a nice person.
--Dave Barry

Blessedly, there is no time off from kindness. Kindness happens *here*, and our lack of kindness can help us see when we're not *here*.

ASSIGNMENT: Today, notice the moments when you are not present enough to be kind.

November 22

My mother said to me, "If you become a soldier, you'll be a general; if you become a monk, you'll end up as the Pope." Instead, I became a painter and wound up as Picasso.
--Pablo Picasso

ASSIGNMENT: Today, practice being thoroughly and completely *you*.

November 23

Don't compromise yourself. You are all
you've got.
--Janis Joplin

ASSIGNMENT: Today, choose yourself in a
situation in which you would ordinarily
abandon yourself. Notice how that feels.

November 24

If we could see the miracle of a single flower, our whole life would change.
--The Buddha

ASSIGNMENT: Today, look for the miracles and really see them.

November 25

Let us not look back in anger or forward in
fear, but around in awareness.
--James Thurber

ASSIGNMENT: Today, can you see that
without a whole world of conditioned,
imaginary meaning neither anger nor fear
would be possible?

November 26

We don't see things as they are, we see
them as we are.
--Anais Nin

ASSIGNMENT: Today, remember that you
are projecting the world you see. (Realize
this with a great deal of compassion for who
you are and how you're growing.)

November 27

I think we all have a little voice inside us
that will guide us. It may be God, I don't
know. But I think that if we shut out all the
noise and clutter from our lives and listen
to that voice, it will tell us the right thing to
do.
--Christopher Reeve

ASSIGNMENT: Today, listen for the little
voice.

November 28

We have two ears and one mouth so we can listen twice as much as we speak.
--Epictetus

ASSIGNMENT: Today, listen for kindness.

November 29

The greatest danger for most of us is not that our aim is too high and we miss it, but that it is too low and we reach it.
--Michelangelo

ASSIGNMENT: Today, pick one thing and aim high.

November 30

Twenty years from now you will be more disappointed by the things that you didn't do than by the ones you did do. So throw off the bowlines. Sail away from the safe harbor. Catch the trade winds in your sails. Explore. Dream. Discover.
--Mark Twain

ASSIGNMENT: Where will you sail today? At the end of the day, write down what you discovered.

December 1

If growing up is the process of creating
ideas and dreams about what life should be,
then maturity is letting go again.
--Mary Beth Danielson

ASSIGNMENT: Today, recognize a conditioned
idea or dream about what life should be,
realize how that limits you, and let it go.

December 2

Difficulties are meant to rouse, not discourage. The human spirit is to grow strong by conflict.
--William Ellery Channing

Where did we get the idea that life should be easy? When did hard work and perseverance become negatives? Perhaps when we stopped delighting in our accomplishments.

ASSIGNMENT: Today, consider all the hard things you've accomplished in your life.

December 3

Make it a point to do something every day that you don't want to do. This is the golden rule for acquiring the habit of doing your duty without pain.

--Mark Twain

ASSIGNMENT: Today, do something you don't usually associate with pleasure and enjoy doing it.

December 4

We are all here on earth to help others;
what on earth the others are here for I
don't know.
--W. H. Auden

ASSIGNMENT: Today, just enjoy all the help
you can give others.

December 5

No one is useless in this world who lightens
the burden of anyone else.
--Charles Dickens

ASSIGNMENT: Today, lighten at least one
burden.

December 6

Only one like myself who has opened his
mouth and spoken, only one who has said yes,
yes, yes, and again yes! can open wide his
arms to death and know no fear!
--Henry Miller

ASSIGNMENT: Today, say yes, yes, yes,
every chance you get.

December 7

Life is like stepping onto a boat that is about to sail out to sea and sink.
--Shunryu Suzuki

ASSIGNMENT: Today, enjoy the ride!

December 8

At the innermost core of all loneliness is a deep and powerful yearning for union with one's lost self.
--Brendan Francis

ASSIGNMENT: Today, let your conversation inside be a welcoming home speech to yourself. Plan a reunion party.

December 9

Only a mediocre person is always at their best.
--W. Somerset Maugham

ASSIGNMENT: Today, aim high and enjoy the effort without a single concern for results.

December 10

People who get nostalgic about childhood
were obviously never children.
--Bill Watterson

ASSIGNMENT: Today, tell all those children
still living inside you what great people they
are.

December 11

Common sense is the collection of prejudices acquired by age eighteen.
--Albert Einstein

ASSIGNMENT: Today, be non-sensical.

December 12

If we cannot be clever, we can always be
kind.
--Alfred Fripp

ASSIGNMENT: Today, enjoy the kindness
that is always available.

December 13

The person who says it cannot be done
should not interrupt the person doing it.
--Chinese Proverb

ASSIGNMENT: Today, decide what you will do
for the love of doing it and do it.

December 14

Our deepest fear is not that we are inadequate. Our deepest fear is that we are powerful beyond measure. It is our light, not our darkness, that most frightens us.
--Marianne Williamson

ASSIGNMENT: Today, express yourself at a time when you usually withdraw or remain quiet.

December 15

When will our consciences grow so tender
that we will act to prevent human misery
rather than avenge it?
--Eleanor Roosevelt

ASSIGNMENT: Today, one tiny act to
prevent human misery⇒perhaps an act of
kindness.

December 16

How beautiful a day can be when kindness
touches it.
--George Elliston

ASSIGNMENT: Today, have a beautiful day.

December 17

You can't live a perfect day without doing something for someone who will never repay you.
--John Wooden

ASSIGNMENT: Today, have a perfect day.

December 18

Live life as life lives itself.
--Zen saying

ASSIGNMENT: Today, stop often, breathe deeply, relax, allow, accept, and enjoy.

Do I contradict myself?
Very well then I contradict myself,
(I am large, I contain multitudes.)
--Walt Whitman

ASSIGNMENT: Today, realize that life is large and can contain a multitude of apparent contradictions.

December 20

A lie can travel halfway round the world
while the truth is putting on its shoes.
--Mark Twain

ASSIGNMENT: Today, move slowly as you
look for truth everywhere.

December 21

The world is so full of possibilities that
dogmatism is simply indecent.
--Albert Einstein

ASSIGNMENT: Today, breathe in the sweet
fragrance of possibility.

December 22

Often I am still listening when the song is over.

--Marquis De Saint-Lambert

ASSIGNMENT: Today, listen for the soft sound of your heart calling you home.

December 23

All that is is the result of what we have
thought.
--The Buddha

ASSIGNMENT: Today, think thoughts of
compassion and kindness.

December 24

What a wonderful life I've had! I only wish
I'd realized it sooner.
--Collette

ASSIGNMENT: Today, take a moment to
realize what a wonderful life you have and
that you don't want to wait a moment
longer to appreciate it.

December 25

From a certain point onward there is no longer any turning back. That is the point that must be reached.
--Franz Kafka

ASSIGNMENT: Today, acknowledge that you have reached that point in your journey home.

December 26

I have found that among its other benefits, giving liberates the soul of the giver.
--Maya Angelou

ASSIGNMENT: Today, find new ways to liberate your soul.

December 27

Our language has wisely sensed the two sides
of being alone. It has created the word
"loneliness" to express the pain of being
alone. And it has created the word
"solitude" to express the glory of being
alone.
--Paul Tillich

ASSIGNMENT: Today, be for a while in the
glory of solitude.

December 28

There is nothing like returning to a place
that remains unchanged to find the ways in
which you yourself have altered.
--Nelson Mandela

ASSIGNMENT: Today, appreciate the many
ways that you have changed over time.

December 29

And the end of all our exploring will be to
arrive where we started and know the place
for the first time.
--T. S. Eliot

ASSIGNMENT: Today, be where you are and
realize you have never been *here* before.

December 30

Let us rise up and be thankful, for if we
didn't learn a lot today, at least we learned
a little, and if we didn't learn a little, at
least we didn't get sick, and if we got sick,
at least we didn't die; so, let us all be
thankful.
--The Buddha

ASSIGNMENT: Today, include yourself in the
"thank you" every chance you get.

December 31

I am always at the beginning.
--The aged Buddha, on being asked what life was like.

ASSIGNMENT: Today, take a long deep breath and *feel* your life beginning.

TALK WITH CHERI

Online Classes

Cheri Huber conducts interactive online classes via e-mail
on a wide variety of subjects
related to Zen awareness practice.
To be notified of future classes
sign up at www.livingcompassion.org.

Open Air Talk Radio

Open Air is Cheri Huber's weekly, internet-based,
call-in radio show.
Find out how to listen and participate at
www.livingcompassion.org.
Hear and download archived shows at www.cherihuber.com.

LIVING COMPASSION

To find out about our work with orphans in Zambia
and about purchasing gift cards and other products
that support that work,
visit www.livingcompassion.org.

* * *

ZEN MONASTERY PEACE CENTER

For a schedule of workshops and retreats and a list of our
meditation groups across the country,
contact us in one of the following ways.

Website: www.livingcompassion.org
Email: thezencenter@livingcompassion.org
Telephone: 209-728-0860
Fax: 209-728-0861

Zen Monastery Peace Center
P.O. Box 1756
Murphys, CA 95247

BOOKS FROM CHERI HUBER
Published by Keep It Simple Books
All titles are available through your local bookstore.
(Distributed by Independent Publishers Group, Chicago)

There Is Nothing Wrong with You	0-9710309-0-1	$12.00
The Key, and the Name of the Key Is Willingness	0-9636255-4-3	$10.00
When You're Falling, Dive	0-9710309-1-X	$12.00
How You Do Anything Is How You Do Everything: A Workbook	0-9636255-5-1	$12.00
The Depression Book	0-9636255-6-X	$12.00
The Fear Book	0-9636255-1-9	$10.00
Be the Person You Want to Find	0-9636255-2-7	$12.00
Nothing Happens Next	0-9636255-3-5	$8.00
Suffering Is Optional	0-9636255-8-6	$12.00
That Which You Are Seeking Is Causing You to Seek	0-9614754-6-3	$10.00
Time-Out for Parents, Rev. Ed.	0-9614754-4-7	$12.00
The Zen Monastery Cookbook	0-9614754-7-1	$16.00
Sweet Zen	0-9630784-4-5	$12.00
Trying to Be Human	0-9630784-1-0	$10.00
Transform Your Life: A Year of Awareness Practice	9780971030952	$14.00

BOOKS ON CD

There Is Nothing Wrong with You on CD	$18.00
The Key, and the Name of the Key Is Willingness on CD	$14.00

To order call 800-337-3040.
Order securely online at www.livingcompassion.org.

Bestseller
from Cheri Huber

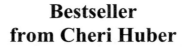

RECARDLESS OF WHAT YOU WERE TAUCHT TO BELIEVE...

THERE IS NOTHING WRONG WITH YOU

REVISED EDITION

COING BEYOND SELF–HATE
A COMPASSIONATE PROCESS FOR LEARNING TO
ACCEPT YOURSELF EXACTLY AS YOU ARE

CHERI HUBER

DESIGNED AND ILLUSTRATED BY JUNE SHIVER

If you are satisfied with what you have been taught about how life works, and if you are content with what society has given you, it would be a waste of your time and money to buy and read this book. However, if you have spent a good deal of time, energy, and money trying to improve yourself, trying to become the person you think you should be in order to make your life work, this is the book for you. We will attempt to explain that you have been unable to fix yourself because there is nothing wrong with you, but there is quite a lot "wrong" with what you were taught to believe about yourself and about life.

Published by Keep It Simple Books
All Cheri Huber titles are available through your local bookstore.
Distributed by Independent Publishers Group, Chicago

There Is Nothing Wrong With You
An Extraordinary Eight-Day Retreat
based on the book
There Is Nothing Wrong With You: Going Beyond Self-Hate
by Cheri Huber

Inside each of us is a "persistent voice of discontent." It is constantly critical of life, the world, and almost everything we say and do. As children, in order to survive, we learned to listen to this voice and believe what it says.

This retreat, held at the beautiful Zen Monastery Peace Center near Murphys, California, in the western foothills of the Sierra Nevada, is eight days of looking directly at how we have been rejecting and punishing ourselves and discovering how to let that go. Through a variety of exercises and periods of group processing, participants gain a clearer perspective on how they live their lives and on how to find compassion for themselves and others.

This work is challenging, joyous, fulfilling, scary, courageous, demanding, freeing, loving, kind, and compassionate—compassionate toward yourself and everyone you will ever know.

For information on attending, contact:
Living Compassion/Zen Monastery Peace Center
P.O. Box 1756
Murphys, CA 95247
Ph.: 209-728-0860
Fax: 209-728-0861
Email: thezencenter@livingcompassion.org
Website: www.livingcompassion.org